بِسْمِ اللّٰهِ الرَّحْمٰنِ الرَّحِيْمِ

In the Name of Allah
The Most Merciful
The Most Compassionate

FROM DARKNESS INTO LIGHT

A. HELWA

Naulit
PUBLISHING HOUSE

contents

the light of mercy..1

the light of faith...33

the light of insight..73

the light of guidance..117

the light of love 153

note from the author

This book is a gentle reminder that divine love is the dawn that breaks every darkness into light. These poems are a soft nudge, reminding you that the glorious rays of God's love can pierce through every veil and illusion. These words are a loving reminder that on the days you feel the soft presence of divine grace, and on the nights you feel hopeless and disconnected—God is with you. God does not leave, even when you struggle in your belief. God loves you, even when you fail to love yourself. God sees you, even when you fail to witness Him. Let this book serve as your reminder that God is with you when you are heartbroken and longing to be whole, when grief weighs heavy on your spirit, and when anxiety shakes your faith. These poems are here to hold your heart both when you begin to trust in the perfection of God's plan for you, and when you are lost in the valleys of your faith searching for guidance in your darkest days.

This book is a reminder that you can be sad and faithful, that you can be broken and grateful, that you can be crawling to God and still graceful. This is a reminder that God expects us to make mistakes and that His mercy makes room for every single heart who sincerely seeks for Him. This is a reminder that you are not defined by your worse faults, by your past, or by who you used to be. Come to God as you are, with your scars, with your broken parts, with your hurting heart, for only the One that made you can save you. After all, being a person of faith does not mean you have a perfect life, but it means that no matter what you face you know that you are always embraced by the love of a perfect God.

A little note to keep in mind as you move through this intimate journey of words: poetic language is not the same as theological language. Not all of these poems can be taken literally. I often use metaphor and similes to point to something beyond the limitations of language. My relationship with the Divine continues to evolve and what I write about in many ways mirrors my personal evolution and aspiration on the spiritual path. Some of these words are imagined, some are inspired, and some are real moments in time. Regardless of the different forms in which these words are presented, one thing is certain, God is one and nothing is like Him, and yet despite His transcendence, He is closer to us than the breath of life within us.

نور الرحمة

THE LIGHT OF MERCY

Look at the delicate petals of a rose,
look at the magic of the bees,
look at the vibrant earth,
its mountains, and its trees.

Look at the galaxies,
at the dancing light of the stars.
Look at the deep blue sea
and the weaving rivers as they part.

Look at the perfect orbit
of every sun and moon.
Look, and see the beauty
of every divine sign
and subtle truth.

Now tell me how you can assume
that God would take care of everything
in this Universe and not take care of you?

Allah knows.

Allah knows how you feel. He knows the secret sorrows you carry. He knows the disappointments and regrets that weigh heavy upon your spirit. He knows the magnitude of your grief. He sees you trying your best. He sees you longing for closeness with Him. He sees your goodness and the places you fall short. He sees the interwoven threads of faith and doubt that embrace your soul. He sees you struggle with temptation. He sees you fight your desires. He hears your shouts. He hears your silence. He hears your call for help and responds to every prayer you make. He is with you every step of the way even if your eyes, ears, and mind cannot capture His presence, He is with you. Allah sees you and His presence is never far, His mercy encompasses you exactly as you are.

Heaven would be empty without God's Mercy.

God sees every tear that falls from your eyes. Even if you cry in the darkness of the night, even if you dive beneath the waves of the sea where your salty tears are imperceptible to human eyes, God sees you. God embraces your pain. God knows what you carry behind the walls of your smile. God is not surprised by your grief, your doubt, and the depression that interweaves like weeds in the garden of your hope.

God chose you for Himself, so God is here to help. God knows how to save you from yourself. God blew into you the mystery of life so that no matter where you are you never forget that He is with you with every breath.

Even if you cannot see God, know that He has never left. God sees every heartbreak, every wound, every scar that you swear will never heal. God sees you from the inside, from beyond the heavens, and through your own eyes.

Nothing you do can ever diminish His mercy for you. His love covers you like the sky and shines upon you like the sun. The doors of His kingdom have no locks so come! Sinner, doubter, the one who has fallen far too many times, come, come!

Allah's love is forgiving.
Allah's love is for giving.

Do not expect from the creation,
what only the Creator is capable of giving you.

In the darkest nights, You are with me.
In the deepest waters, You are with me.
In the hardest seasons, You are with me.
In my doubt filled days, You are with me.
In my worst heartbreaks, You are with me.
In my heaviest depression, You are with me.
In my fearful anxiety, You are with me.
You are with me in every moment of every day.
You are with me in sickness and in health, in life and in death.
In every success and every failure, You are with me.
Even when I am not with You, You are always with me.

The storm will pass.
The sunny skies will pass.
The ease will pass.
The difficulty will pass.
The happiness will pass.
The sadness will pass.
Nothing will last, except for His Grace.
Everything is passing away, except for His Face.

Allah is the only One that can use the things that hurt you to heal you.

I am praying with the wind tonight. I pray that the wild breeze allows you to see, that through God's Will unseen forces can move you to exactly where you are meant to be. As you watch the leaves dance to music that cannot be heard, I pray you begin to hear God's speech without the need for words and lines. You are special to the Divine. I see it in your pain, in the ways you are being broken...open.

The hurricanes of trials that you face, the oceans of sorrow falling from the clouds of your eyes is a way that God clears your vision and turns you to Him. When you have nowhere else to turn to but God, it is a gift. When you let go of everything, but God that is when you will see who you are. You are not this body, this identity, this persona that masks a spirit that is far beyond pictures and pigments.

You are energy in the disguise of dense form. You are a fragrance of forever living in the finite. You are so much more than your mind can grasp in its limited timeline. Words lose meaning when duality collapses. Who is speaking when time no longer passes? Who is listening when you speak when only He exists? If words no longer have space to travel, what becomes of language here? I whisper because God is near. I no longer speak because God is here. I have never felt more alive than when I dissolve in the presence of the One who gave me life. I live my life chasing the death of all attachments. To disappear in the presence of God is to be alive forever. I pray that you always remember that you and God are always together.

Do not trust your eyes to remind you of the light. All life begins in darkness, in wombs, in soil, in cocoons. No matter what you face, what burdens you carry and what monsters your fears create, know that you are being embraced in the loving light of His mercy and grace. Know that you are in God's hands. Just know that everything is going perfectly according to God's plan.

God did not bring you this far just to abandon you now. The God who brought you to this moment is the One that will guide you through it.

Trust in Him.

God has bigger plans for you.

You are not alone. Even if it feels like you are an island surrounded by an endless horizon of waves, you are not alone. Even when it feels like the night has swallowed all the light you held inside of you and the moon has turned away from the sun so the world has no light to give to you, you are not alone.

Even in the shattered pieces of your past that rose into canyons of scars on the valleys of your skin, you are not alone. When the world has broken your heart, you are not alone. When no one seems to understand or see you, you are not alone. God is with you wherever you are, you are never alone.

Stop running. Stop running from the God who surrounds you with His love. Like a fish trying to swim away from water, wherever you run, you will only run into Him. No matter where you go, God is there. His love embraces you even in your anger, rage, and hate. He loves you more than your mistakes. He loves you more than your fears. You can run, but He says, "I am near." Even on the days you say you do not believe, He never leaves. You can run, but He never leaves.

His love knows no border, no veil, or separation based on color or country. Allah is bigger than your religion, your thoughts, than all of your limiting ideas of God. Allah loves the spirit of your soul more than infinity can hold. Allah is the essence of everything you reach for and everything that you seek. Allah is the origin and destination of all peace.

I dance in the silence of infinite mercy and its endlessness embraces me with gentleness. I am floating upon the rivers of destiny rushing softly toward the ocean of eternity. Forever awaits me in a future that is now and here already.

I am a blossom. I am a seed shattering. I am flowering. I am a wave rising. I am a volcano bubbling. I am the beginning. I am the forever new. I am the disappearing dew drop swallowed by the sun's glow. I am the cloud's tears being kissed by light into a rainbow. I am the in-between. I am the dream between wakefulness and sleep. I am the soul that is unseen.

I am the melody of paradox. I am a nothingness before God. I am this nothingness. Oh how sweet emptiness feels when you are fertile soil awaiting the seed of divine inspiration.

My soul is its highest when I'm aware that Your mercy encompasses everything. My Lord, please allow me to live to my fullest potential from a place of surrender. Lord help me to honor Your gifts, but to not be attached to what I am given.

My Lord, open my heart and allow me to be generous in sharing the blessings you have bestowed upon me. Let me love this life, but love You more. Let me remember that I am a wave and this life is just a shore. In time I will be pulled back into the ocean of unity and return back the spirit You once blew in me.

Remember: God does not live in you, but you are alive because of the life He gives to you.

Whatever Allah removes,
He replaces it with something
better for your soul.

We all have moments
when we turn away from the truth,
don't judge someone for sinning
in a color different than you.

—*it is human to make mistakes*

Allah is embracing you in every single moment.

He will never leave your side. He is closer to you than the life in your veins and closer than the breaths that wash over you like waves coming and going from the shores of your lips. When everyone else leaves, when every dream breaks, when every hope shatters, He is still there. His love will never break your heart. His friendship will never expire. He will always have your best interest at the tip of the pen of His Decrees. He writes only what is eternally beautiful for you and your journey.

When Allah loves you, He only breaks you to heal you.

He only takes from you to give you what is better for your soul. He only closes one chapter to write you a new one. Your story has more pages than the one you are on. Your story has more characters, more victories, and more treasures for you to find. Know that every page you lived through led you to this moment, to these words because Allah also wrote for you to read this, for you to be reminded that He is here for you. He sent love letters through His prophets, peace and blessings be upon them, to guide you back home, back to the infinite ocean of love that all earthly rivers of compassion and kindness return to. Hold onto the rope of Allah for the roots of His love will keep you grounded through the storms of this life. Hold onto Allah for no one will ever love you more than the One who blew a spirit of light into you to give you life.

Do you know who you are? You are a reflection of heaven on Earth. Do you know who you are? You are the chosen representative of an exalted God.

God is always speaking, but frequently
our ears are not tuned to His frequency.

You are not defined by your worst sins.
The past is meant to be learned from
not meant to be lived in.

When it comes to Allah's mercy,
no sin is too big to forgive.
When it comes to Allah's generosity,
no deed is too small to reward.

You are the One that is with me through every storm I have ever faced. You are the One who is with me in the tornado of my thoughts that tangle me in the webs of fear, anxiety, and expectation. You are my ark, when my mind is a hurricane drowning my heart with a flood of falsehood and fantasies.

You are with me on the darkest nights of my soul. When the world feels broken and I feel alone, You are with me, perfect and whole. When those who I loved have passed, when those who I loved have left, when those who I loved have broken my heart, Your love surrounds me like oxygen. You are with me with every step. You are with me with every breath. You never leave. Even when I didn't believe in You, You stayed with me. There is no moment void of Your love.

There is no place empty of Your presence. You are the King who rules the Universe and You are the Lord of every electron that dances within my cells. You saved me more than a billion times from myself. You are the One who can never be thanked enough. You are the Origin of love.

You are the invisible hands that hold the birds up, the One who calls the sun and moon to swim in orbits in the sky. You are the architect of the day and the night. You are the Creator of light. You give hope to the fearful and hopeless. You are the Most Loving, the Most Merciful, the Most Great. You are Allah and nothing in this world is like You, and yet everything in existence points to Your Presence, which is beyond time and space.

Words fail to capture Your grace. Words fail to give You shape. You are Allah, the One that breaks the mind and makes the hearts whole. You are Allah, the One who blew the gift of life into my soul.

—*forever bewildering*

Allah is the only One you need to please.

—*the path to peace*

When God gives us more than we think we can handle
He is calling us to rely on Him in a deeper way.

—*the hidden mercy of pain*

When God heals you, don't go back to the person that hurt you. When God frees you, don't go back to the prisons that enslaved you. When God awakens you with His light, don't go back to the darkness that kept you asleep. When God speaks to you, don't go back to listening to your ego. When God welcomes you, don't go back to the spaces your spirit never belonged in. When God forgives you, don't go back to the same sins. When God says you are priceless, don't go back to thinking you are not good enough.

Remember: God sees you, He hears you, He loves you more than infinite universes of countless spinning stars. When the whole world tells you who you should be, remember, God welcomes you exactly as you are.

When you heal the wounds inside you,
it changes the way you see the world around you.

We only judge in others
what we fail to recognize in ourselves.

—*you need a mirror to see your reflection*

The scars I carry are not flaws,
they are like signatures from God,
reminding me that I am stronger
than the things that once threatened
to destroy me.

Sometimes God has to ruin your plans
to redirect you toward your true purpose.

نور الايمان

THE LIGHT OF FAITH

You may have prayed for a star,
but Allah may have had universes destined for you.

You may have longed for the fragrance of a flower,
but Allah may have had eternal gardens destined for you.

You may have desired for the tiniest drop,
but Allah may have had infinite oceans destined for you.

Whatever you may want,
know that Allah wants better for you.

As the sun rises into a new day,
Lord, transform the darkness
of my soul through dawn
of Your love.

Awaken the sun of faith within me
and brighten my soul with the light
of Your presence.

My Lord, purify my soul, until I am the eyes by which You see, the hands by which You embrace, the tongue by which You speak, the feet by which You steer, and the ears by which You hear. My Lord, make me empty of me and a mirror for You.

My Lord, use me as a refuge for my sisters and brothers, use me to answer the prayers of others. Make me a shelter for those without a home and a companion for those who are isolated and alone.

My Lord, use me however You wish, as an embrace of love and as a hand that gives. Oh Lord, make me dust upon the path You have paved, make me a mirror of Your loving grace.

—*ameen*

I am tired of these winters that do not seem to go away,
I want to force this seedling of faith to time lapse into
something I am proud to see today.

—*impatience*

If you keep digging up the seeds you sow,
nothing you plant will ever grow.

—*tawakkul*

My Lord,
if it doesn't evolve my spirit,
then don't involve me in it.

—*growth focused*

My Lord, protect me from any success that will turn my heart away from You. My Lord, protect me from any failure that will turn my heart away from You. Remind me that if I gain the world, but lose You I have nothing but illusion in my possession. But if I lose the world and gain the witnessing of You, I have lost what is perishing in exchange for You, who are forever and eternal.

Remind me that my preferences do not determine what is good or bad for my soul. Remind me, that when my heart turns to You, whether it be through a trial or a blessing, it is always good. And remind me that when my heart turns away from You, whether it be through a trial or a blessing, that it is always bad.

My Lord, remind me that what is with You is always good and what makes me forgetful of You is always bad. My Lord, keep my heart in witness of You. My Lord, keep my eyes aligned to You. My Lord, from the womb to the grave, keep my spirit always in the remembrance of Your names.

Patience is not about waiting until all your prayers come true, it's about surrendering to whatever God has written for you.

I step onto the prayer mat, and the world around me begins to collapse. I am standing upon the waters of possibility as the sweet sea of existence flows beneath me. Time and space have no place to hold, this is the realm of the soul.

This breath I breathe originates from a holy fragrance that language cannot make into a perfume and sell. The mystery of life is a secret pearl hidden in an invisible shell. Nothing can capture a Lord who transcends everything, yet Allah is here in this moment with me.

You say prayer is how we speak to Allah, but I say prayer is when our ego disappears and only Allah's speech is heard. Allah is always speaking, but only sometimes do we hear His words. Allah is always raining His love upon us, but only sometimes do we remove the lids from our cups. Allah is always forgiving us, but only sometimes do we choose to forgive ourselves. Allah is always near, but only sometimes do we ask for His help.

We turn away from Allah because of our own fears, and then complain why Allah disappeared. We close our ears and shut our eyes and then argue Allah's love is conditional because we are blind in the night. The sun doesn't die when the Earth turns its back on its light.

Allah does not stop loving you because you stopped receiving His love within. Allah does not stop existing, because you stopped believing in Him.

Allah has already perfectly worked out every little thing that you are busy worrying about.

I pray that you find corners of silence in your busy day to let the light in, to feel the breeze, and to look toward the stars hidden beneath the rays of the sun. I pray you make time to take in the blue sky, to dive into the crystal seas, to breathe in the emerald trees, and perfume your senses with the scent of roses and jasmine.

I pray you remember that the beauty of everything you see is a reflection of God's majesty. You are alive because of a God who continues to blow the breath of life within you. God's speech projected life upon the canvas of nothingness through the light of His love. God loves us in the language of colors, in the beauty of shapes, in divine signs and all that is hidden that lies between the lines. God loves us through everything we see. God loves us through everything we cannot see.

Everywhere we turn to from the east to the west, the face of God is all that we see even when we fail to recognize the sacredness beneath the disguise. If you are blinded by literalism, you will call this blasphemy. If you are drunk on pride and say *there is only one way that is right and it happens to be mine* then you will be blinded by your idea of the Divine.

God is bigger than your eyes, and bigger than your "I". He is bigger than your mind. God encompasses every moment, we are never alone. God is with us wherever we are, we are already home. Heaven is where you and God are together. Heaven is there, Heaven is here, Heaven is everywhere you choose faith instead of fear.

When my sorrow tangles my tongue and my feelings are too heavy to lay on the backs of words, that is when I cry. These tears that I hide are a language that only God speaks. So I stand on my broken faith, and I come with my mountains of mistakes because I have nowhere else to go.

Who can heal me better than the One who formed my soul from the tenderness of His love?

Like a broken cloud that rains upon the dirt, my pain overflows past the edges of my eyes upon the earth where I prostrate to the only One who knows exactly how I feel. When I do not have the words, but still need to be heard, I fall into the love of Allah. He is always there for me. Like the sky that covers everything, He is there.

His Mercy has no end for He is the Friend that will never leave, the One whose name alone brings my heart the peace it so desperately seeks.

The old keys we have may not open the new doors we encounter, but the prayers we have said a thousand times can dissolve the walls in our way.

—*the weapon of the believer*

Dear Allah,
Thank you for believing in me
even when I didn't believe in You.

Every single moment we are desperately dependent on God. Not just when we need something from Him, not just when we pray, not just when we are grateful.

Every single breath we take is a choice God makes. We are alive because God intentionally chooses for us to be here. The God of existence, of the celestial spheres, the expanding Universe, and changing seasons chose us and continues to choose us.

How can a God so big, put so much care and mercy into a creation so small? How can we, who came from nothing, be loved so tenderly? How can we be so forgetful of God, when we need everything from Him? How can He lovingly remember us, when He needs nothing from us?

When the world breaks your heart,
pray for Allah's healing.

When anxiety overwhelms you,
pray for Allah's grace.

When darkness envelops you,
pray for Allah's light.

When loneliness surrounds you,
pray for Allah's presence.

When negative thoughts fill your mind,
pray for Allah's protection.

When you can't let go of the past,
pray for Allah's mercy.

When you feel anxious about the future,
pray for Allah's peace.

No matter what you face,
pray for Allah's mercy and loving grace.

When you prostrate before Allah,
you can stand before anyone.

There is an infinite difference between knowing
God is watching you and God is watching *over* you.

You can whisper God into your prayer beads endlessly and wear robes perfumed with faith, but love does not awaken in words alone. Love cannot be captured by religion. Love is not something man can interpret. Love is too grand to fit on a path of cobblestones and intentions. Love transcends the grasp of the intellect. It is beyond where the seen and unseen intersects, yet it weaves through every molecule we breathe. Everything speaks of love, but love cannot be held in letters and it cares little for poetry. Put the best words in the best order, and you cannot write love. Love is beyond language, but surrendering with love is the only path to God.

Worship through love leads to freedom and peace. To love is to let go of the ego and be dissolved in the Divine. Devotion without the death of the lower self means nothing, for in duality and separation love cannot be made. Love is where there is no you and no I, where there is no space and no time. Love lives where everything collides. Love lives where we escape the limitations of labels and signs.

We are in love even when we are searching for love. We are drowning in love even when we are thirsty for love. Love is always near, for love is the reason that we are here. Love is the silence that holds meaning in its palms. Love is the fragrance of the rose, and yet love is the rose, soil and sun, and everything in between. Love is awake even when we dream. Love lives where life cannot reach. Love walks where paths are not paved. Love walks where death's blade cannot kiss love's feet.

Love may bleed, but love does not leave. Love may weep, but love does not grieve because love knows no distance, and love knows no separation. Love can only know love, to understand love is to become love, so love with your whole heart until love is all you are.

Darkness embraced me with its hands, slowly tightening its grip, attempting to extinguish the dawn that lives within me until no light exists.

But darkness did not know that my light is not my own. Like the moon is a mirror that reflects the sun, I reflect an eternal God whose light perfumes every soul.

Darkness will come and go, but my God will never leave, for He is closer to me than every breath of life that I breathe.

The best part of speaking to your Lord is knowing He can hear your silence even when you can't put your feelings into words.

My Lord,
I am in desperate need
of every ounce of goodness
that You send down to me.

When you change the statement,
"I have to pray" to "I get to pray"
your relationship to your faith
will begin to transform.

Wherever you are and whatever you feel know that Allah is with you. You don't have to wait to be perfect or flawlessly faithful before you seek Him. Speak to Him with your voice of sorrow, pain and brokenness. For better or for worse, call out to the Origin and Source of love in this Universe. Come with your imperfections, broken trust, doubt, and even your disbelief. After all, where else will you find refuge if it is not with the Most Merciful?

Allah is here.

When you close your eyes and the world disappears, He is here. When everyone else leaves, He is here. When you call His name, He is near. Do not grieve, do not fear.

Call Him by His names, He is here.

When anxiety makes it hard to breathe, when the voices in my mind get the best of me. When my regrets from the past take me back in time, when memories of heartbreak awaken in my mind. When everything hurts, when everything feels broken and nothing works. When my faith feels like a candle facing a tornado wind, when the devil keeps taking wins. When darkness envelops my heart and makes me blind, when the peace I am searching for I just can't find. When I have nothing to give, when I begin to lose the will to live. When I do not feel worthy of calling Your Name, when I am drowning in an ocean of shame, like sunshine in the rain, that is when You came.

You arrived in my life and everything changed. Your love is greater than the storms that I face. You had never left, but my eyes were closed. Now with every breath, I feel a river of hope. Your love is moving within me, but You are not contained by me. I am an echo that follows the words of Your plan. This Universe cannot reflect You the way the mirror of our hearts can.

We are chosen to represent Your love on Earth. Your spirit makes us into gardens from dead dirt. This breath that gives me life came from You and yet forms cannot capture Your Truth. Only the blind would say you are far too infinite to feel intimate, Your light pierced the soil of my skin and reached into it, deep within me into the seeds of peace that You planted. Peace comes from You, it must be granted. Lord, please grant it. Allow us to not forget that Your light never sets.

Lord, help me to let go of everything in my life that does not help me grow. Lord, help me see that no matter what I want, You are the only One I need. Lord, help me remove every idol in the way that prevents me from witnessing Your Face. In Your infinite names, I pray, I pray, I pray!

On my best days, Allah give me gratitude. On my worst days, Allah give me patience. When I am blessed, Allah make me generous. When I am wronged, Allah make me forgiving. When I am struggling, Allah make me persevere. When I am anxious, Allah give me peace. When I am heartbroken, Allah heal me. When I sin, Allah forgive me. When I am lost, Allah give me guidance. When I am in darkness, Allah give me light. When I see others sin, Allah protect me from the eyes of judgment. No matter what I face, Allah make it a means for turning my heart toward Your names.

Our thoughts have creative power. We see creation through the lens of our interpretations. Existence is a mirror, so when we change the way we think about the world, our experience of the world changes.

We do not see the world as it is, but rather as we translate and interpret it to be.

Be conscious of your thoughts for they are vibrations that turn into waves. Your thoughts are prayers you knowingly or unknowingly make.

Prayer changes destiny.
Prayer can change who you thought you were destined to be.

I fell to my knees distraught with my dying need for Allah to reply to me. I prayed, "My Lord, I have known Your name since before I could spell mine. I have given You decades of my life in pursuit of Your truth. Where have You been, Lord? Why won't you speak? Why won't you acknowledge me?"

The silence enveloped me from behind, embracing my soul and my mind. I fell into a dream that came outside the grasp of sleep. My spirit ascended into a space between realms where I could no longer speak.

In the silence, I heard an angelic voice say from beyond the veil, "Allah loved you before you had a name or shape or any form at all. You may have loved Him for a lifetime, but Allah loved you before time itself."

We bring God our emptiness and He responds with His fullness. God buys our lack, our poverty, and all of our nothingness at the price of His infinite everything.

I pray Allah shows you how to grow through
the trials that He has written for you to go through.

Who would you be if you let your faith guide you instead of fear?

Dear Allah,

I am in desperate need of Your help. Please do not leave me to myself for even the blink of an eye because my eyes are blind without You by my side. In the darkness, I cannot see, it is Your light that bestows sight upon me. Lord, I made mistakes in my words and actions, but You are the cause of all good that happens. You take my sins and make me into seeds; with Your forgiveness You make a garden out of me. Lord, do not give me what I deserve, do not judge me based on what I am worth. Give to me based on Your generosity, not my deeds. Cover me in the cloak of Your Mercy! Protect me from the voices of the darkness that curse me. Protect me from my own ego that tries to hurt me. You are my one refuge, my only safe place. Return me again and again to the straight path of Your timeless grace.

When what you prayed for does not come true, know that Allah is protecting you. Allah brings to you what is best for you. Our minds cannot solve the equations of divine math, but we must trust in the answers that Allah has. Do not always depend on the intellect you can grasp, rely on Allah to have your back. Trust that when the time is right, Allah will bring to light what is best for you.

Talking about God is not the same as talking to God.

I asked Allah for strength so He sent me trials. I asked Allah for growth so He sent me rain. I asked Allah for freedom, so He showed me the prison of my ego. I asked Allah for patience, so He made me wait. I asked Allah for answers, so He filled me with questions. I asked Allah for love, so He took away the world and gave me Himself.

نور البصيرة

THE LIGHT OF INSIGHT

Just like a baby seed buried in the Earth, being nurtured into a tree, by the love of a sun it cannot see, God's light is changing you in ways that cannot always be seen.

I say I have no time for You, yet You created time for me.

—*perspective*

Is the air in a bowl different from the air that surrounds it? Is the breath of life inside of me different from the breath of life inside of you? The sun makes the plants green, roses red, and the sky blue, but the light that unveils all color is one. Fire makes water into steam, ice into liquid, and wood into ash, but the heat is one. The outcomes are countless, but the Origin is one.

—*attempting to see unity with two eyes*

How much longer will you carry the burden of their mistakes? Forgive them. Even if they never apologize, forgive them. They may not deserve your forgiveness, but you deserve the peace and healing that comes through forgiveness.

I get so caught up in what I own and what I'm owed
that I forget that I myself am a loan.

—*copyright Allah*

You carry a sun inside that never sets.

—*ruh*

You are not living *inside* the Universe,
you *are* the Universe.

Do not risk forever for the fleeting pleasures of this moment.

Does what you own, own you?

—*attachment*

I do not know what tomorrow holds,
but I know in Whose hands my future is held.

If your heart has a pulse, your life has a purpose.

—*you were intentionally created*

The sun never leaves, it is the earth that turns away.

—*the darkness is a veil*

Trying to understand God through the mind
is like looking for the sun with a flashlight.

—*finite hands cannot hold infinite realities*

Allah is greater than the storms that blow your way. He is greater than the depression, anxiety and heartbreaks you face. Allah is greater than the pain. He is greater than your sins, your addictions, and silent suffering.

Allah is greater than the abuse, than all the hurtful words that have been said to you. Allah is greater than the loneliness you feel and the hopelessness that follows you.

Allah is greater than your mistakes. He is greater than the misperceptions the world has about you. He is greater than your shortcomings, your broken promises, and your failed commitments. Allah is greater than the love of your life, than your children, than your family and friends. Allah is greater than the influence, the fame, and the fortune.

Allah is greater than this world, this galaxy, and this entire Cosmos. Allah is greater than you and greater than me, yet He still makes time for us. He still loves us. He still forgives us. He is far too great for existence to embrace, yet He still chooses to be closer to us than our jugular veins.

—*Allahu Akbar*

Sometimes I am too embarrassed to ask God for help because I can't find the words to express the universe of feelings that spiral inside of me. Sometimes there is no language to grasp all that I am lacking. Sometimes I forget that my silence is a prayer, that my need to be heard is still a need even when I cannot paint it with words.

I turn to You my Lord, with all the spaces between words that give language meaning. I pray with all of my silence. I give You all the words I do not have. You, who have created everything from nothing, create something beautiful from the nothing I have to offer You.

Our breath connects us across time and space. This single breath that blows through us makes us family. Your exhales travel through me and with me. Your breaths become me. My breaths become you. When we breathe, we breathe in millions of molecules of air that once swirled inside of the prophets. Our breaths carry the past and connect us with what once was. With every breath we embrace loved ones that have passed, and every single creature that ever breathed on this planet from now into the past. Separation is an illusion. Breathe in deep and remember you are breathing air that touched the life of everything in existence.

—*one soul*

Every single person that I meet
has a message from God for me.

—*divine carrier pigeons*

We never know which person, place, or plan is best for our hearts, but we trust that there is goodness in whatever Allah has written for us.

An alternative to gossip: pray behind people's backs.

The things you shame and judge in someone else,
are the unhealed wounds you carry inside yourself.

—I hate in you the parts of myself I am unable to love

The mirror does not own what it reflects.

Bear in mind, this entire world you will leave behind.

—*impermanence*

When you die you return to Him.
Death is your homecoming, not your going away party.

—*a doorway to eternity*

God said, "Be" and existence flowered into being without a single seed.

The Pen is one, but the shapes are many.
The Breath is one, but the words are many.
The Light is one, but the colors are many.
The Soul is one, but the creatures are many.
The Divine is one, but His names are many.

—*singularity hides in multiplicity's disguise*

You are everywhere.

You cannot be contained in the creation You chose to create, but I still see Your face reflected in the Universe You molded into shape. I see You from the stars to the seas to the blades of grass and bumble bees, from the rivers to the mountains and their peaks, from a lover's gaze to a babies laugh, from the parting of seas to the golden calf, from the prophets across time to the revelations and divine signs, from the human heart to the human mind, from the unseen to all that the eyes can touch, from separation to the embrace of love. I see You through loss and grief to the freedom of peace, from the broken to the whole, from the body to the soul, from the angels to the devils, from the sun that rises to the sun that settles, from the moon that waxes to the moon that wanes, from the guided to the lost, from my emotions to my thoughts, from the palaces of the past to kingdoms to come, everything and everyone is a reflection of the One.

Everything is a manifestation of Your speech, so if I am shy when I speak, if my voice shakes when I talk of the stars and the waves, it's because everything I see from the east to the west is a picture of Your face. Everything is a ceremony. Everything is prayer. Everything is sacred. What can be profane if existence only draws me to Your name? What can be taken from me, what can I lose, when everything takes me back to You? My shadows point to the light. You are the only One that never leaves my side even when I cannot catch You with my eyes. You never leave. I run away from You, only to run into You. Your omnipresence is the ultimate truth.

The journey is from You, to You, with You. Separation is an illusion. Other than You, does not exist. Literal eyes cannot make sense of this divine disguise. Literal minds fail to see that without Your face the mirror of existence would fail to be. You are the giver and taker of life; everything exists because of Your Light.

This world is a bridge we are meant to walk across
not meant to worship.

The different flowers in the garden
speak with countless colors of the same sun.

—infinite shapes point to one Name

Everything you see is painted with light.

—*Nur*

Your beauty comes from God.
You are a divine design manifested
into being through the hands of love.

Your shape is held with the scaffolding
of bones and cloaked with soft skin,
but your body is not your home,
just the vehicle you were sent in.

—*you are more than the eyes can capture*

We are both human so why can't you see
that nothing you say or feel could ever be
entirely alien to me.

—*from one soul*

Whatever happens in your life
was the best possible outcome
for you to get closer to Allah.
Trust in Allah's Decree.
It was never meant to hurt you,
it was meant to set you free.

—*qadr*

When the fruit is ripe, it will fall.

—*trust in God's timing*

Winter comes, stealing your blossoms with the blade of time,
but don't forget within your winter that spring is close behind.

—*hope*

I am nostalgic for a home I do not remember.

—*Paradise*

Our inability to witness God is due to our limitations not due to His lack of presence.

—to the eyes of a bat, the sun is dim

There is one God,
but infinite perceptions of Him.

—we see the Divine through filtered eyes

My heart doesn't beat, like a compass it spins
from God to this world and then back to Him.

—*qalb*

Sometimes we are so blinded by a good opportunity that we miss the God opportunity.

Do not be hurt when someone calls you only when they are in need, be grateful that you are the sun they seek when darkness steals their peace.

Be the sun.
Be the North Star.
Be a lifeboat.
For the broken and the lost,
be a flame that lights hope.

نور الهدى

THE LIGHT OF GUIDANCE

Stop and take a moment to breathe.
Inhale.
Exhale.
Feel the power of your breath.

Remember:
you can breathe through everything in life, but death.

You are different than your father. Your purpose here is different than his. You are different from your mother. Your purpose here is different than hers. We were not created from earth, light, and sacred breath just to manifest our parent's unfulfilled dreams. Our fathers and our mothers are not God. They are our earthly foster parents whose bodies adopted us.

We belong to God and in time we will return to Him. We were not just created to worship God and to reflect His qualities of beauty and majesty, but each of us has a unique talent we were sent to this Earth to manifest. We must respect our parents and their dreams for us, but we are not obligated to follow their plans for our lives.

We must break the idols we have unconsciously created of our parents for we are commanded to obey God alone and His commandments above all others. We must be careful to not take our parents as idols before God.

We were not sent here to make our parents proud,
we were sent here to please God.

Let go of everything you identify with yourself. Let go of your personality and your learned responses based on your past experiences. Let go of your name, your culture and the society that raised you. Let go of your job title, your accomplishments, your past, and your hope for the future. Let go of being human, of your body, of your entire existence.

You are not what people call you. You are not what you do. You are not the color of your skin or the religion you follow. Let go of every pigment of identity, until you are a blank canvas of infinite possibilities. Until you are free from the heavy adornments of the ego.

Now look. Look without eyes at yourself. Look at the eternal beauty you carry that space and time cannot hold. Look at your divinely inspired, mysterious soul. Look beyond your flaws. Look at how you are a mirror for the love of God.

Earthquakes must arrive before mountains can rise. Sometimes things have to shatter and break before they can be recreated in a new way.

—breakdowns come before breakthroughs

Do not steal the opportunity of others to work on themselves. Sometimes out of the desire to protect those we love we run the risk of preventing them from receiving the lessons and teachings they need most to grow.

The process of transformation is painful. We cannot endure that pain for someone else any more than one caterpillar can endure the pain of the cocoon for another caterpillar to become a butterfly.

We need to be careful that our compassion and love for others does not end up preventing them from being planted in the uncomfortable, yet fertile soil of growth.

Remember: Allah does not give anyone a burden greater than they can bear.

Do not be so attached to your expectations of the future that you become ungrateful for the blessings God has given you in this present moment.

What you see as good and bad are based on your preferences of what you think you need or wish you had. The path God paves for you is not based on your comfort and ease, but based on what will help you grow the most on the path toward peace.

Avoid over-analyzing.
Acknowledge your feelings.
Ask Allah for help.

—*the path to healing*

Instead of asking, *Why did this happen to me?*
Ask God, *What do You want me to see?*

When hardship finds you don't waste time asking, *Is this a test or am I being punished?* The response is the same—turn back to Allah and pray for His unconditional mercy and eternal grace.

Do not keep tripping over what is already behind you.

—*let the past go*

To be inspired is to be a tree blossoming in spring.

The rush of love floods through my veins like colors of light bursting into life. This sacred breeze is a breath, this divinity flows like rivers through the Earth taking every heart to the ocean through the gravity of devotion.

My pen is a boat here, it is not the current. My pen is a sail here, it is not the wind. What I write is a shadow that the light casts. I am not the voice, but the echo that bounces off the mountains of existence. When the mountains are kissed with the glance of God, they become sand. I swoon into the sleep of love where Moses is my captain, but we are both surrendered to God's plan.

Here between the two seas of death and dreams, I am awake. I am love-drunk so what I sing does not come from my mind. Nothing makes sense here, but everything feels right. In the center of the black hole of my poverty, I feel safe because my neediness allows me to receive His grace. God is letting me access a truth that I can't understand, but my heart can taste. God has no form or shape, and yet still everything sings of His face. Every letter is a mirror of His name.

So, what can I say that is void of His grace, when every word I say begins first with His pen on His page?

—*maktub, it has been written*

Our ideas of God are not God.

Our interpretations of God's revelation are not revelation. We must be careful not to mistake the streams and rivers of our thoughts for the ocean of Truth. The Divine is not a butterfly that can be caught with a net of the mind.

What we see as *interruptions* in our lives are really *interventions* from the Divine calling us towards deeper connection with Him.

What triggers us is a doorway of return to God because our triggers illuminate our attachments. It is through being given awareness of our attachments that we can surrender to God. After all, we cannot give up what we fail to recognize exists. The world cannot make us angry or happy, but external forces can shine light upon the anger and joy that live within us. Anger is not just an emotion, it is an interpretation of a moment. Anger can be a signal of deep sadness, a boundary being crossed, a sign that our feelings are hurt, or a symptom of not being heard or seen with holiness and compassion. Our emotions are not mindless, they are rooted in real experiences.

We react to life's different situations based on our past interpretations and beliefs. If our reaction to an experience seems extreme or exaggerated, it is often an indication that we are responding to unhealed wounds from our past rather than just the present situation.

The gift of our emotions is that they point us toward an attachment or belief we have held onto and need to relinquish. Our attachments are like cataracts when we remove them the light of truth penetrates our spiritual vision allowing us to witness God with more clarity.

—*let go and let God*

The world can either be a distraction from Allah
or a doorway to Allah.

—*the choice is yours*

Be careful what thoughts you sow
within the fertile soil of your mind.
You become a graveyard or a garden
depending what you bury inside.

If a boat is anchored to another boat, eventually both boats would get lost. To find stability and security we must anchor to something that is not fleeting, that is stable, and fixed. Boats anchor to the seabed, a port, a mountain, or to something that is rooted. It is only when you anchor yourself to Allah that you will be unaffected by the changing tides of this fleeting world.

Darkness and light cannot coexist. If everyone loves you, you may be a hypocrite. Sometimes people's criticisms are the greatest forms of praise. You cannot stand up for the oppressed and be liked by their oppressors at the same time. Do not be afraid of being disliked by some people, be afraid of being liked by everyone.

How will you ever find yourself
when you're so lost in someone else?

Enlightenment doesn't happen in a day, it happens daily. You see a seed sprout suddenly from the soil, but the tree of faith has been growing for a long time before your eyes capture its blossoms. Can you trust in God's process? Can you trust that God is doing something in your life even on the days you cannot measure the change?

May the knowledge you acquire
either lead to certainty or bewilderment.
God is experienced most brilliantly in the truth
and in the places where our minds fail to travel to.

The sun will continue to shine,
even if the entire world goes blind.

—*God's existence is not dependent on your belief in Him*

Why do we overemphasize God speaking to us in an audible form? God doesn't need language or air for sound to travel through in order to speak to you. God can blossom thoughts, feelings, insights and realities deep into your heart and mind without the constraints of language. Light does not need to touch your eyes for God to show you the truth. Your mind doesn't need to translate light into electrical signals to see the faces of the Divine. Your ears don't have to transform waves of sound into a language the mind can speak for you to be able to hear God's guidance. The Divine can skip the line of your senses and speak directly to your heart in a language beyond the limiting form of words.

Why do we need to hear God's audible voice to believe in His existence? We don't require the devil's voice to be audible, but can acknowledge the feeling of being tempted. When the devil speaks to us we call that temptation and when God speaks to us we call that inspiration. Inspiration simply means being in spirit, in connection with something beyond just ourselves that calls us to our essence.

God is speaking to us. God is responding to us. When we fail to hear God it's not God who has gone silent, it is often we who have stopped listening.

The seed has to undress itself of the shell of its limitations to become a tree. You have to let go of who you have been to become who you were destined to be.

—*let the dead leaves fall*

Follow your heart *only* when it is purified and aligned to God. Following our heart when it is enslaved to the mind, makes us act from our preferences rather than God's prescriptions. An impure heart is one that is attached to this world, and ruled by the desires of the ego self. Just because we feel a certain way doesn't justify acting on that feeling. May we not allow our fleeting feelings to dictate our future, but rather let the principles of our faith determine our future.

Do not become attached to the ways God revealed Himself to you in the past. How you saw God yesterday, can become a veil in our experience of His presence today. God transcends time and escapes the constraints of space so we cannot grasp Him with the limited mind. Infinity cannot be captured by a being who is stuck within the constraints of time. Divine signs hide behind subliminal lines.

God's Word inspires existence to be birthed from nothingness into a living Universe. God is everywhere and His love is reflected in everything. The soft touch of His light resurrects the dead earth every spring. You cannot see Him, but it is because of His light that you can see. He created the entire world by uttering, *Be*—and suddenly everything was. In an instant, all of existence blossomed from His love.

Do not judge people when they act in a way that is not in alignment with the divine laws of love, instead be grateful that Allah opened your heart to the awareness of Him and blessed you with the gift of guidance. When you see someone follow the laws of Allah with more excellence and sincerity than yourself, do not be envious. Instead, be grateful that the Divine has inspired your heart towards longing for greater connection with Him. No matter what you witness in creation, let it be a reminder of the Creator's mercy upon you, rather than a means of judgment upon others.

Some days my pen feels like a leaf
being blown by the winds of Decree
into shapes unbeknownst to me.
I write faster than I can think,
letting my ego drown and sink
beneath the waves of inspiration,
that flow in ink.
Like an audience waiting for what is next,
I watch in amazement at how God's breath
moves me to write a pattern of words
my brain could never create,
and yet I sign *my* name.
When God said, "Be"
He wrote what I will echo into existence,
so I just wait to receive.

This paradox is hard to understand.
You and I are not prophets,
but nothing can happen outside of God's Plan.
There is a hidden mystery in all that we choose,
as God's mercy encompasses everything,
including me and including you.
All inspiration and beauty belong to God alone,
so how can I take credit for what I write as my own,
when everything I am given from God is a loan?
Whatever good comes from me belongs to Him.
I breathe in His love to exhale these rhymes,
again and again, I write with the Divine
on my heart and on my mind,
And although my name is signed,
know these words are not mine.

—*the preserved tablet*

Contemplate the book that you are writing. What needs to be added to the story of your life before your book is handed back to the Creator Who gave you its pages and its ink? What will the story of your life say to the One who wrote for you to witness His beauty in everything? Every time you breathe, the letters of life find their way to eternal pages of sacred tablets. Like the stars spill their light upon the dark scrolls of the night, every step you take, every action you make, and every word you speak is written by angelic scribes on the pages of space and time. So if today was the day that you died, would you be happy with the book of your life?

—*deadline pending*

I know that you are hurting.

If you were looking for a sign or a divine reminder
that Allah loves you, let this be your sign. Have faith.
Allah knows what you are going through and He is
with you every step of the way.

Just like water appears as the color of the vessel it's held within, your life mirrors the color of your intentions and thoughts.

Worship while you wait
for everything to fall into
its perfect place.

—*faith*

There is one word that can change your whole life. This word can transform your relationship with Allah, restore your hope and increase your commitment to faith beyond what you could imagine. It is the three lettered word, *yet*. You have not healed *yet*. You have not become the type of person you want *yet*. You are not where you want to be in your relationship with Allah *yet*.

Keep striving, keep walking, keep seeking Allah, and know that He is with you and the best is *yet* to come.

نور المحبة

THE LIGHT OF LOVE

I sit in the fire of Allah's love where every form and shape of distinction and separation burns away. On the path of transcendence every idol shatters and breaks. I sit in the fire of Allah's love where my tears of pain are revelations of grace. In this love, every heart becomes fertile soil and every eye becomes a pregnant cloud whose sorrow of separation sings in the melody of rain. Through worship the seeds of faith burst into life through the kiss of divine gentleness and light.

I am broken like bread, I am broken like night into the day, I am the type of broken that blossoms flowers from the shells of my limitations that God's love begins to break. The spark of devotion has caused wildfires in my soul and nothing can breathe in this surface sun of heat except for love. Nothing else can co-exist with the One who has no opposites.

Every pain I have ever faced came from forgetting Your Name. Spending lifetimes turning toward myself in shame or toward others with blame in search of the peace that only emanates from Your Presence. My Lord, I plead and I ask that You surround me with the flames of Your love until everything but You becomes ash, until my idols become my past, until my ego disintegrates and something new emerges from beyond my masks. Lord, I sit in the blaze of Your love and fan the flames with the breeze of prayers on my tongue. Lord, I sit in the fire of Your love until all of me melts away and all that remains is nothing but Your Face.

Love bewilders the mind and tangles the tongue.

Language is a martyr of love.

Like a shadow vanishes in the presence of the sun,
in love there can never be two, there can only be One.

When I disappear,
You appear.

—*God is always near*

I am a nothingness that Allah molded into existence
with the breath of His divine love and mercy.

How can I bargain with the Merchant of everything? I bring You counterfeit goods and You purchase them with gold. I bring You my teardrops, and You give me an ocean. I bring You dust and You offer me the Garden. I bring You myself and You award me with Yourself. How can my nothingness be so valuable? How can my emptiness be so priceless?

I have gone mad from this divine math. Every hair on my head has grown into a thousand buds of blooming roses, each singing in fragrant notes of Your love. You buy my zeros with eternity. You buy my dying breaths with forever. If justice is receiving what I deserve, then You are beyond the very definition of the word. You bestow upon me infinitely more than I could ever earn. Your love breaks all my scales.

Every passing day I am more aware that human language cannot capture Your eternal generosity. Words are dead soil, nothing eternal can grow in the letters mouthed by my mind without Your mercy behind every letter. It is only from Your speech that universes sprout from the created garden of time. It is only from Your words that out of nothingness there is form. It is only from Your love that we are formed.

What is there to say about the One who created speech? What is there to give to the Creator of everything seen and unseen? Silence seems to be the only path in expressing a mystery beyond what the mind can map. It is only in the silence that infinity can be expressed because once words are employed infinite possibilities collapse into finite forms, but You cannot be held in the limiting hands of language. I cannot reach Your Essence through these rhymes and letters, it is in the empty spaces between the words that I find we are together.

—*beyond the mind*

Your love choreographs my tongue into words I swear I do not know how to speak. Your love makes poems out of the chaos inside of me. Your love makes music out of the silence. What can I say when Your love has me tongue tied, tripping over myself, falling in love with You.

—*falling out of me and into You*

Do not fall in love with the gift,
fall in love with One who created it.

The moon would disappear into the night,
if the sun stopped kissing her with its light.

—*I am because You are*

I did not fall in love, I fell inside of His Love. And now I cannot find my way out. I lost my borders, my body, and my hands, so now I have nothing to grasp, nothing to touch. In the face of Love, I disappear. Time lives, but I am no longer here. God speaks and I hear, but I listen with no ears. God is alive, but I am dead. I am a sleeping seed inside the breath of a divine *Be* that will one day undress nothingness and burst me into being from the womb of empty space.

Do you see the heavens in my face? Do you see the divine constellations engraved in our souls? Our hearts carry the map back to the sacred home we left so long ago. Do you see how forever holds time in its embrace? Do you see God—how He is everywhere I am not? Do you see God's plan—how He is everywhere I am? Do you see how God is reflected inside, outside, and beyond space, how He is not limited by the creation He chose to create? Do you see how there is so much more than you can see? Do you see how your eyes are blind to capture the divinity hidden beneath the seams of the unseen?

We are blind to the light that surrounds us all the time. We are dreamers that have yet to wake, fighting voices that we ourselves create. The ghosts of our past are given shape by our fears, but these shadow puppets would disappear if only we turned on the light of Love. The sun of Truth will rise again, washing the darkness from our eyes. In time, you will see everything exactly as it is, as it will be, and as it was. In time, you will see that every atom dancing in and out of time is just another face of Love.

The world broke my heart, but God broke my heart *open*.

The difference between these two heartbreaks is greater than infinite universes of ink could grasp.

When God breaks a seed open, it blossoms with flowers. When God breaks a cloud open, it rains. When God breaks an egg open, life emerges. When God breaks a cocoon open, a caterpillar is given wings.

Not all breaking is the same. When we turn to God with our broken hearts, He opens us to realities beyond our greatest imaginations.

The beauty of existence is breathtaking, but if I fail to witness Your Presence, it doesn't drop me to my knees. It is the essence of Your love that illuminates every shape that I see. It is the way Your mercy embraces me when I am in need. It is the way Your Presence mends my heart when it is desperate for peace. It is the way Your kindness braids into every word that You speak. It is the way Your patience is unending for sinners like me. It is the love You give when I don't deserve a single drop, that makes me fall to my knees, and declare, You are the most generous God.

You are a poem made of star kissed bones instead of words. Your blood is the ink that paints the clay pages of an ancient book that can't be heard. Your heart carries the soul of love that every poets pen is after, a melody of mystery that language fails to capture.

—you are the living word of God

I can't take my heart off of You.

I am drowning in an ocean of His love within.
A place where only those who die can swim.
I die to myself like a snake sheds its skin.
I am born again and again just to drown
into the ocean of His love within.
Only those who die can swim,
so I die a thousand times in Him.

—*die before you die*

Like a compass is moved by the Earth's poles, the love of the Divine attracts my soul. God pulls me in like gravity, as I am lifted toward the sky without strings or ladders for love defies the eyes.

Love makes every grave into a garden. The kiss of divine light makes everything blossom. The death of the lower self is fertilizer for life like darkness is the canvas for light. Death is not an end, but a new face of a new beginning that time cannot chase. Forever is beneath the veil of our last exhale. When the boat of the spirit sets sail into the ocean of the unknown we harvest all the love that we once sowed. We are unveiled of our bodies and embody a single soul. The righteous stand before rivers of milk and honey dressed in silk and gold.

As we let go of everything we are not, our spirits dissolve like snow into the light of God. We are finally here, in the forever where time cannot reach. We are finally here, where the heart finds rest and the soul lives in eternal peace.

—*Jannah*

God is with you always and in all ways.

I could feel the earth holding me as I walked, calling my body towards the same dirt that once formed me. The branches of the trees swayed as they shaded me from the piercing sun's heat. The ground kissed my feet with every step. The fragrant breeze embraced me with every breath.

This is how nature shows me she loves me.

Nature was mothering me. Mother Nature is a womb I was born into from my mother whose body was the soil for the seeds God spoke into existence. The clouds cry for me and the earth replies to me with roses that bloom. The sun dives into the sea and leaves behind a piece of itself for me in the mirrored moon. Everything I see is a way that God speaks to me. Nothing is void of Him. He is reflected in the furthest stars scattered across the night sky. His love is mirrored from the ends of the horizon to the universes that swirl deep inside.

—*He is with you always*

Be with someone who is good for your spiritual health.
Someone who does not just make you fall in love with them,
but inspires you to continuously fall in love with Him.

God loves you, even if they don't like you.

Divine light shines its gaze upon me, and its light unfolds me like a flower, a prayer, a lover. It loves me pretty. It loves me to death. I die in the arms of the light and its rays take me to the origin of all Light. My shadows cannot exist in His radiant Presence. The light makes no room for darkness.

All that I am dissolves away. I cannot speak. I cannot hear. I cannot see. Because here in the unity I had to leave myself behind to come inside. But I feel God more in this death than I ever could living in a dream I called being awake. Death…it is the thing I run from only to run into. God has not punished us with death, but rewarded us with it. It's your ticket home, but you cannot force it just like you cannot force the seasons to arrive before their time. The seed has to be planted when God decides. It is in the death of the seed when the tree can rise.

Surrender to God's timing.

Listen to the spring of Paradise sing of how fruitful it is to leave behind the limitations of mortal human time and trust in the eternal Divine. You can only reach God with God. No vehicles of clay and earth can reach the One who has no shape. His love gazed at the mountain of Moses and it swooned into sand for how could its ranges bear eternal love in its stony hands? If you want to know God you have to give up your mind because the mind sees the world through opposites, but God is one. To know God, you have to give up your truth to receive His Truth.

The price of knowing God is you.

You are everything I see and everything I am blind to,
from the east to the west wherever I look I only find You.

—*Allah*

Love is the overflowing presence of God
that awakens existence into being.

It is love that brought us here.
It is love that sustains and embraces us here.

It is love that will take us back home.
From love we came and to love we will return.

Our journey on Earth is not just to God,
it is from God, with God, and into the love of God.

Your flaws will never greater than the love of God.

Watching you search for Love is like watching a fish
seek for the water it already lives within.

—*omnipresence*

If any part of your heart is closed toward accepting
His creation, then your heart can not be fully open
to the Creator.

I burn with a love inside for the Divine like I am the melting sun. The fires of this world feel like a cold breeze when I am with the One.

You are not defined by what you are going through.
In your deepest moments of pain and loneliness
God's love is embracing you.

You cannot outrun Allah's love for you.

How can the God whose love makes every atom twirl with life inside of you not intimately know how you feel? God sees your sadness and He holds your heart with gentleness and delicate mercy.

God sees the parts of yourself you fight to hide. God sees you from the inside, outside, and beyond time. God embraces your loneliness, walks beside your grief, and heals the parts of your heart you swore could never be whole again.

When everyone else leaves, God stays. When no one else notices the hidden burdens of shame and regret that you carry, God sees you. He loves you for His mercy forgives all sins. He is with you even when you are not with Him.

I do not know what the next chapter will bring, but I know it's been written with love by the greatest Author there ever will be or ever was.

—*Allah*

about the author

A. HELWA believes that every single person on Earth is deeply loved by the Divine. She is the author of the internationally bestselling book, *Secrets of Divine Love: A Spiritual Journey into the Heart of Islam*, which is currently available in English, French, German, Arabic, and Turkish. Learn more about her work and how to approach the Divine through love online at @a.helwa_ or www.authorahelwa.com.

a few last words

Remember, we were born in the womb of the stars. We are made of celestial light and earth. We eat the sun. We breathe the breath of the trees. Our breaths mingle with the leaves, with each other, with the swaying tides of the seas. We carry oceans inside of us and galaxies are born every time God speaks through His Decree. We are part of the wind that lifts the wings of the birds and the bees. We are neither here nor there. Through these divine breaths we travel everywhere. We are not static. Our breath plays an ever-changing melody through the instrument of our bodies. Every moment we are a new song. We are always changing. We cannot be held in one shape or feeling that time keeps stealing. We are impermanent.

If I say these hands are me, I have lied, because if you take my hands I am still me inside. If I say these feet are me, I have lied, because if you take my legs I am still me. This body I see in the mirror is just a vehicle, a canvas that holds the paint of God's masterpiece of life. The clouds don't belong to the sky. The stars don't belong to the night. The sun does not belong to the horizon it rises upon. Everything we see is just passing through, so why would it be different with me or you?

CPSIA information can be obtained
at www.ICGtesting.com
Printed in the USA
LVHW112028281122
734147LV00021B/303

9 781957 415031